The McGraw-Hill Companies

McGraw-Hill
Irwin

STATISTICAL TECHNIQUES IN BUSINESS AND ECONOMICS
Published by McGraw-Hill/Irwin, a business unit of The McGraw-Hill Companies, Inc., 1221 Avenue of the
Americas, New York, NY, 10020. Copyright © 2008 by The McGraw-Hill Companies, Inc. All rights reserved.
No part of this publication may be reproduced or distributed in any form or by any means, or stored in a
database or retrieval system, without the prior written consent of The McGraw-Hill Companies, Inc.,
including, but not limited to, in any network or other electronic storage or transmission, or broadcast for
distance learning.

Some ancillaries, including electronic and print components, may not be available to customers outside the
United States.

This book is printed on acid-free paper.

1 2 3 4 5 6 7 8 9 0 WCK/WCK 0 9 8 7 6

ISBN   978-0-07-303022-7 (student edition)
MHID   0-07-303022-8 (student edition)
ISBN   978-0-07-303023-4 (instructor's edition)
MHID   0-07-303023-6 (instructor's edition)

Editorial director: *Stewart Mattson*
Executive editor: *Richard T. Hercher, Jr.*
Developmental editor II: *Christina A. Sanders*
Marketing manager: *Sankha Basu*
Senior media producer: *Victor Chiu*
Project manager: *Jim Labeots*
Production supervisor: *Debra R. Sylvester*
Senior designer: *Adam Rooke*
Photo research coordinator: *Kathy Shive*
Photo researcher: *Jennifer Blankenship*
Supplement producer: *Ira C. Roberts*
Media project manager: *Matthew Perry*
Typeface: *9.5/11 Helvetica Neue 55*
Compositor: *Techbooks*
Printer: *Quebecor World Versailles Inc.*

Library of Congress Cataloging-in-Publication Data

Lind, Douglas A.
   Statistical techniques in business & economics / Douglas A. Lind, William G. Marchal,
Samuel A. Wathen. — Thirteenth ed.
      p. cm. — (McGraw-Hill/Irwin series operations and decision sciences)
   Includes indexes.
   ISBN-13: 978-0-07-303022-7 (student edition: alk. paper)
   ISBN-10: 0-07-303022-8 (student edition: alk. paper)
   ISBN-13: 978-0-07-303023-4 (instructor's edition: alk. paper)
   ISBN-10: 0-07-303023-6 (instructor's edition: alk. paper)
   1. Social sciences—Statistical methods. 2. Economics—Statistical methods. 3. Commercial
statistics. I. Marchal, William G. II. Wathen, Samuel Adam. III. Title. IV. Title: Statistical
techniques in business and economics.
HA29.M268 2008
519.5—dc22

2006018157

w.mhhe.com

Student CD contains:

MegaStat® for Excel®
Getting Started with MegaStat® for Excel® (User's Guide)
Visual Statistics
ScreenCam Tutorials
    Excel®
            Introduction
            Regression
    MegaStat® for Excel®
            Introduction
            Descriptive Statistics
            Regression
    Minitab
            Introduction
            Regression
Self-Grading Practice Quizzes
Data Sets
    Excel®
    Minitab
    SPSS
Data Files
    Excel®
    Minitab
PowerPoint
Weblinks
    Online Learning Center
    Chapter References and Internet Exercises
    Business Statistics Center
    ALEKS®
    Homework Manager™

Statistical Techniques in
Business & Economics

Thirteenth Edition

Douglas A. Lind
Coastal Carolina University and The University of Toledo

William G. Marchal
The University of Toledo

Samuel A. Wathen
Coastal Carolina University

**McGraw-Hill
Irwin**

Boston   Burr Ridge, IL   Dubuque, IA   Madison, WI   New York   San Francisco   S
Bangkok   Bogotá   Caracas   Kuala Lumpur   Lisbon   London   Madrid   Mexic
Milan   Montreal   New Delhi   Santiago   Seoul   Singapore   Sydney   Taipei

The McGraw-Hill/Irwin Series
Operations and Decision Sciences

Business Statistics

Aczel and Sounderpandian
Complete Business Statistics
Sixth Edition

ALEKS Corporation
ALEKS for Business Statistics
First Edition

Alwan
Statistical Process Analysis
First Edition

Bowerman and O'Connell
Business Statistics in Practice
Fourth Edition

Bowerman and O'Connell,
Essentials of Business Statistics
Second Edition

Bryant and Smith
Practical Data Analysis: Case Studies in Business Statistics, Volumes I, II, and III*

Cooper and Schindler
Business Research Methods
Ninth Edition

Delurgio
Forecasting Principles and Applications
First Edition

Doane
LearningStats CD-ROM
First Edition, 1.2

Doane, Mathieson, and Tracy
Visual Statistics
Second Edition, 2.2

Doane and Seward
Applied Statistics in Business and Economics
First Edition

Gitlow, Oppenheim, Oppenheim, and Levine
Quality Management
Third Edition

Kutner, Nachtsheim, and Neter
Applied Linear Regression Models
Fourth Edition

Kutner, Nachtsheim, Neter and Li
Applied Linear Statistical Models
Fifth Edition

Lind, Marchal, and Wathen
Basic Statistics for Business and Economics
Fifth Edition

Merchant, Goffinet, and Koehler
Basic Statistics Using Excel for Office XP
Third Edition

Olson and Shi
Introduction to Business Data Mining
First Edition

Orris
Basic Statistics: Using Excel and MegaStat
First Edition

Sahai and Khurshid
Pocket Dictionary of Statistics
First Edition

Siegel
Practical Business Statistics
Fifth Edition

Wilson, Keating, and John Galt Solutions, Inc.
Business Forecasting
Fifth Edition

Zagorsky
Business Information
First Edition

Quantitative Methods and Management Science

Hillier and Hillier
Introduction to Management Science
Second Edition

Kros
Spreadsheet Modeling for Business Decisions
First Edition

Stevenson and Ozgur
Introduction to Management Science with Spreadsheets
First Edition

*Available only through McGraw-Hill's PRIMIS Online Assets Library.

To Jane, my wife and best friend, and our sons, their wives, and our grandchildren: Mike and Sue (Steve and Courtney), Steve and Kathryn (Kennedy), and Mark and Sarah (Jared, Drew, and Nate).

Douglas A. Lind

To Elizabeth and William, the most recent additions to our family.

William G. Marchal

To my wonderful family: Isaac, Hannah, and Barb.

Samuel A. Wathen

Preface

The objective of *Statistical Techniques in Business and Economics* is to provide students majoring in management, marketing, finance, accounting, economics, and other fields of business administration with an introductory survey of the many applications of descriptive and inferential statistics. While we focus on business applications, we also use many problems and examples that are student oriented and do not require previous courses.

The first edition of this text was published in 1967. At that time locating relevant business data was difficult. That has changed! Today locating data is not a problem. The number of items you purchase at the grocery store is automatically recorded at the checkout counter. Phone companies track the time of our calls, the length of calls, and the number of the person called. Credit card companies maintain information on the number, time and date, and amount of our purchases. Medical devices automatically monitor our heart rate, blood pressure, and temperature. A large amount of business information is recorded and reported almost instantly. CNN, *USA Today,* and MSNBC, for example, all have websites where you can track stock prices with a delay of less than twenty minutes.

Today, skills are needed to deal with a large volume of numerical information. First, we need to be critical consumers of information presented by others. Second, we need to be able to reduce large amounts of information into a concise and meaningful form to enable us to make effective interpretations, judgments, and decisions.

All students have calculators and most have either personal computers or access to personal computers in a campus lab. Statistical software, such as Microsoft Excel and MINITAB, is available on these computers. The commands necessary to achieve the software results are available in a special section at the end of each chapter. We use screen captures within the chapters, so the student becomes familiar with the nature of the software output. Because of the availability of computers and software it is no longer necessary to dwell on calculations. We have replaced many of the calculation examples with interpretative ones, to assist the student in understanding and interpreting the statistical results. In addition we now place more emphasis on the conceptual nature of the statistical topics. While making these changes, we still continue to present, as best we can, the key concepts, along with supporting examples.

The thirteenth edition of *Statistical Techniques in Business and Economics* is the product of many people: students, colleagues, reviewers, and the staff at McGraw-Hill/Irwin. We thank them all. We wish to express our sincere gratitude to the survey and focus group participants, and the reviewers:

Reviewers

Sung K. Ahn
Washington State University–Pullman

Pamela A. Boger
Ohio University–Athens

Giorgio Canarella
California State University–Los Angeles

Anne Davey
Northeastern State University

Nirmal Devi
Embry Riddle Aeronautical University

Clifford B. Hawley
West Virginia University

Lloyd R. Jaisingh
Morehead State University

John D. McGinnis
Pennsylvania State–Altoona

Mary Ruth J. McRae
Appalachian State University

Jackie Miller
Ohio State University

Elizabeth J. T. Murff
Eastern Washington University

René Ordonez
Southern Oregon University

Joseph Petry
University of Illinois at Urbana-Champaign

Michael Racer
University of Memphis

Darrell Radson
Drexel University

Christopher W. Rogers
Miami Dade College

Stephen Hays Russell
Weber State University

Martin Sabo
Community College of Denver

Amar Sahay
Salt Lake Community College and University of Utah

Nina Sarkar
Queensborough Community College

Gary Smith
Florida State University

Stanley D. Stephenson
Texas State University–San Marcos

Lawrence Tatum
Baruch College

Daniel Tschopp
Daemen College

Jesus M. Valencia
Slippery Rock University

Joseph Van Matre
University of Alabama at Birmingham

Kathleen Whitcomb
University of South Carolina

Blake Whitten
University of Iowa

Oliver Yu
San Jose State University

Survey and Focus Group Participants

Nawar Al-Shara
American University

Charles H. Apigian
Middle Tennessee State University

Nagraj Balakrishnan
Clemson University

Philip Boudreaux
University of Louisiana at Lafayette

Nancy Brooks
University of Vermont

Qidong Cao
Winthrop University

Margaret M. Capen
East Carolina University

Robert Carver
Stonehill College

Jan E. Christopher
Delaware State University

James Cochran
Louisiana Tech University

Farideh Dehkordi-Vakil
Western Illinois University

Brant Deppa
Winona State University

Bernard Dickman
Hofstra University

Casey DiRienzo
Elon University

Erick M. Elder
University of Arkansas at Little Rock

Nicholas R. Farnum
California State University, Fullerton

K. Renee Fister
Murray State University

Gary Franko
Siena College

Maurice Gilbert
Troy State University

Deborah J. Gougeon
University of Scranton

Christine Guenther
Pacific University

Charles F. Harrington
University of Southern Indiana

Craig Heinicke
Baldwin-Wallace College

George Hilton
Pacific Union College

Cindy L. Hinz
St. Bonaventure University

Johnny C. Ho
Columbus State University